A MINI GUIDE TO
ROCK CLIMBING

WRITTEN BY
Matt Stieb

ILLUSTRATED BY

RP Minis®
Hachette Book Group
1290 Avenue of the Americas, New York, NY 10104
www.runningpress.com
@Running_Press

First Edition: September 2024

Published by RP Minis, an imprint of Hachette Book Group, Inc. The RP Minis name and logo is a registered trademark of Hachette Book Group, Inc.

Running Press books may be purchased in bulk for business, educational, or promotional use. For more information, please contact your local bookseller or the Hachette Book Group Special Markets Department at Special.Markets@hbgusa.com.

The publisher is not responsible for websites (or their content) that are not owned by the publisher.

Design by Jenna McBride

ISBN: 978-0-7624-8765-3

Contents

Introduction

ROCK ON,
ANYWHERE YOU WANT!

◆◆◆

Rock climbing is great, but once you start, you never really stop thinking about it. After you've felt the highs of getting to the top of a route that once felt totally impossible, you can't help but imagine the moves to a climb while at school or at work. Pretty soon you'll be miming the actions in the air, confusing your friends and loved ones.

At last, there's a solution to all that. When you can't get to the crag or the gym, get out the Finger Rock Climbing kit and set up a mini version of the route you can't stop thinking about, right at your desk. And while you're keeping the psych up, learn a bit more about the never-ending lingo and the history of the sport, from the medieval days to the impossibly hard stuff the pros are climbing today.

FINGER ROCK CLIMBING GUIDELINES

◆◆◆

Like with real climbing, there aren't too many rules—aside from the all-important safety ones. Get the climbing shoes snug on your fingers, be your own route setter, and find out the most challenging and creative ways to get to the top!

The History of
Rock Climbing

People have been summiting mountains as long as humans have existed, but the technical practice of getting up a vertical rock face might have begun as early as the 1400s, when a French military engineer used his knowledge of storming over castle walls to summit a 300-foot cliff in south France.

The discipline as we know it today began in the 1800s, when Europeans across the continent began taking on the steepest stuff they could find. To keep themselves safe, climbers invented pitons to hammer into the wall to attach their rope to. (If you're on a classic climb, you might run into them still today.) Over the next 100 years or so, mountaineers from Italy, France, Germany, and England pushed themselves up increasingly difficult routes, developing new gear and methods.

After World War II, Americans began to show their stuff. Thanks to the nylon ropes invented during the war, falling became safer and climbers at Yosemite National Park established some of the greatest climbs the world has ever seen. The next few decades told a story of climbers running into technical problems, inventing what they needed to excel, then climbing even harder when they got their hands on the new tools. The

experts ditched the piton for a combination of little brass squares called nuts and spring-loaded devices called cams to keep them safe—a combo known as a trad kit today. On their feet, the fashion evolved from heavy boots to rubber high-tops to sticky rubber slippers that could gain purchase on even a tiny nubble. As the climbing difficulty went up, the discipline of sport climbing was born: to access steep overhanging rock that trad gear could not protect, climbers began putting bolts in the rock to push themselves to the very limit of what the human body could do. By the end of the century, people were climbing routes that were impossible for the early innovators to get halfway up.

In the last few decades, thanks to the rise of climbing gyms, the practice went from a relatively niche sport only available to those living in mountain areas to a form of exercise available to anyone who's not afraid of heights. A breakthrough moment came in 2016, when climbing joined the Olympics and was broadcast to fans around the world.

The Wide World of Climbing Lingo

Anchor The piece of metal at the top of a wall that a climber ties into to complete a route.

Belayer The person on the ground who safely feeds the climber rope as they go up; a friend to catch you if you fall.

Beta The way to complete a climb. The term comes from Betamax, an old type of cassette video that climbers would film themselves on back in the day.

Cam A spring-loaded device that looks like a metal fist that trad climbers squeeze into cracks and attach the rope to for protection if they fall.

Chalk In the 1950s, a gymnast turned climber named John Gill realized that gymnastic chalk would keep his hands dry while climbing, improving his grip on small holds. Now, it's a standard in every climber's kit.

Crimp Using the tips of your fingers to pull onto a really small hold on the rock.

Crashpad The foam blocks climbers take into the woods to protect them when they fall while bouldering.

Crag The local cliff for climbing.

Choss Rock quality that sucks. It's crumbly and unreliable and usually isn't much fun to climb on.

Deep water solo Climbing without a rope over a body of water deep enough that if you fall in with good form it won't be dangerous.

Dirtbag Someone, most often living in a van, who has dropped the real world for the climbing one. It's more of a badge of honor than an insult.

Dyno A dynamic move where you leap off the wall to get to the next hold.

Elvis leg When you're worried about falling while high in the air and your legs begin to shake uncontrollably.

First ascent The first time someone climbs a route. The first ascensionist gets to name it and establish the grade.

Flash To complete a route the first time you try it.

Free soloing Climbing high into the air without a rope. We here at Finger Rock Climbing would advise you not to do this.

Harness The device you wear around your hips to attach yourself to the rope.

Jug A huge hold that is easy to hang onto and is a relief to come across on a hard route.

Knee bar Jamming your knee into a large piece of rock to allow your arms to rest.

Mantle The muscle-intensive move where you go from pulling down to pushing up to get over the top of a boulder.

Nut Little brass squares that trad climbers place into small cracks to protect themselves if they fall.

Project The climb that you're working on slightly above your current skill that you try many times to get to the next level. Also known as a proj.

Quickdraw A small sling with carabiners on both sides that sport climbers use to clip their rope into the wall for safety.

Rappel The method to descend the rope after you get to the top.

Route setter The person who sets the problems in a gym—or on the Finger Rock Climbing wall. That's you.

Sandbagged When a climb is way harder than it says it is.

Sending Successfully completing a climb without using a rope to rest.

Sloper A bad hold that is difficult to hold onto.

Whipper A giant fall.

WHICH TYPE OF CLIMBING IS FOR YOU?

◆◆◆

BOULDERING

The introductory style in most gyms, bouldering does not involve a rope. Instead, climbers jump on a foam pad on the ground after finishing a short route called a "problem." It's notoriously fun and ranges from the easiest stuff around to some of the hardest climbing in the world. The grading system ranges from V0 to V17, with each grade increasing in difficulty.

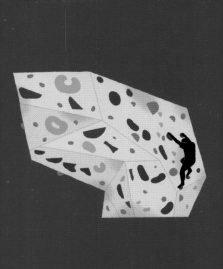

The intro to rope climbing involves a rope coming down from an anchor at the top of the route, which allows the climber to avoid falls: when you let go, you hang in the air right where you left off. For rope climbing in the United States, the grades range from about 5.5 to 5.15D. Each grade also gets incrementally harder.

SPORT CLIMBING

In this discipline, climbers clip into bolts on the wall to keep themselves safe as they ascend. But if you fall, you go down twice the distance above the last bolt.

TRAD CLIMBING

Trad climbers bring their own gear and place it in cracks on the wall to keep themselves safe as they go up. Generally, there's no such thing as indoor trad climbing, and it requires much more technical expertise about knots and gear. It's scarier and more adventurous but does allow for big wall climbing like the stuff you see in Yosemite.

The Dos and Don'ts

◆ **Be responsible.** Even low-to-the-ground climbing has a level of danger. It's up to you and your climbing partner to safely know how to belay and use your gear properly to make sure everyone gets down on the ground safely.

◆ **Clean up after yourself.** If you're climbing outside, bring any trash back to the car with you.

◆ **Challenge yourself.** Climbing is most rewarding when you're pushing yourself past what you once thought imaginable. On the other hand, don't push yourself too much—getting in over your head is potentially dangerous.

DON'T:

◆ **Walk under other climbers.** At the gym or at the crag, it's rude and dangerous to get in the immediate zone of other groups while they're up in the air.

◆ **Give too much advice.** Many climbers are happy to hear the beta on a certain climb, but for others, figuring it out is the fun part. If you've already done a route, make sure to ask before giving other people tips.

◆ **Get too frustrated.** As you advance
   up the grades, climbing can get really
   hard, really quickly. To get better,
   you'll want to push yourself, but
   getting bummed out about not
   sending rarely helps.

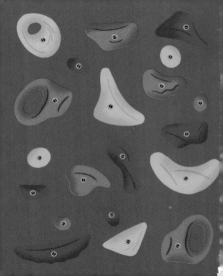